THE OFFICIAL
TOTTENHAM
HOTSPUR
ANNUAL 2015

Written by Michael Bridge
Designed by Brian Thomson

A Grange Publication

© 2014. Published by Grange Communications Ltd., Edinburgh, under licence from Tottenham Hotspur Ltd. Printed in the EU.

Photography ©Action Images

ISBN: 978-1-908925-73-2

WELCOME...

Contents

Dear Supporters,
Welcome to the 2015 Official Tottenham Hotspur Annual.

We finished sixth in the Barclays Premier League last season, securing European football once again at White Hart Lane.

It was a season of what might have been, our seven signings needing time to adapt to a new league and country. We finished on 69 points – our third-best Barclays Premier League tally. 14 clean sheets was our joint-highest in the Barclays Premier League and 21 wins was also our joint-best.

We are now in an exciting new era under Head Coach Mauricio Pochettino who took over in May, 2014, and arrived at the Lane with a glowing reputation as one of the most progressive young coaches in Europe.

In the following pages, you'll find a comprehensive 2013/2014 Season Review and an in-depth look into our squad, plus the rising stars of the Lane. Meet our new signings, test yourself in the quiz section and find out just why we are unique. Remember, in a world of Uniteds, Citys and Rovers... there is only One Hotspur.

Enjoy your new Annual. **Come on you Spurs!**

PREMIER LEAGUE REVIEW

2013/2014

Tottenham Hotspur secured another top six finish in the Barclays Premier League, which guaranteed European football for the fifth successive season.

There were many positives to take from last season, notably the form of Christian Eriksen and a second consecutive victory at Old Trafford, having previously not won there since December 1989.

AUGUST

Pld: 2 W: 2 D: 0 L: 0
End of month League table position: **third**

Tottenham Hotspur started the season with a trip to newly-promoted Crystal Palace. All eyes were on our new-look squad, as Roberto Soldado, Paulinho, Nacer Chadli and Etienne Capoue made their debuts. Soldado scored a 50th minute penalty after Aaron Lennon's cross was handled by full-back Dean Moxey. Tottenham Hotspur did not win a penalty in the whole of the 2012/2013 Season, but were awarded their second in as many games after Swansea's Jonjo Shelvey brought down the lively Andros Townsend. Six points from two games was the perfect start. Christian Eriksen, Vlad Chiricheș and Club record signing Erik Lamela arrived to take the total new signings to seven. Gareth Bale completed his world record move to Real Madrid.

SEPTEMBER

Pld: 4 W: 2 D: 1 L: 1
End of month League table position: **second**

A first half goal from Olivier Giroud settled the first North London derby of the season at the Emirates. Two goals from Gylfi Sigurdsson sealed a 2-0 win against Norwich at White Hart Lane. Christian Eriksen impressed on his debut. Eight days later Tottenham Hotspur travelled to Cardiff, scoring a deserved stoppage time winner after dominating throughout. Paulinho scored his first Premier League goal. We finished the month with a 1-1 draw at home to Chelsea. Sigurdsson again on target. John Terry levelled for Chelsea.

OCTOBER

Pld: 3 W: 2 D: 0 L: 1
End of month League table position: **fourth**

Our unbeaten home run came to an end after a 3-0 defeat to West Ham which saw the Hammers leave White Hart Lane with three points. We responded with a comfortable 2-0 win at Aston Villa. Andros Townsend, fresh from scoring for England, was the man of the match. Roberto Soldado was also on target. Soldado was the match-winner again after an 80th minute penalty against Hull was enough to secure three points for Spurs at home.

NOVEMBER

Pld: 3 W: 0 D: 1 L: 2
End of month League table position: **ninth**

A 0-0 draw with an impressive Everton side was the best moment in a disappointing month. An outstanding goalkeeping performance from Tim Krul helped Newcastle United win 1-0 on a frustrating afternoon at White Hart Lane. A 6-0 defeat to Manchester City at the Etihad followed, which saw us finish the month in ninth position.

DECEMBER

Pld: 7 W: 4 D: 2 L: 1
End of month League table position: **seventh**

December was a month of change at White Hart Lane. It started with an entertaining 2-2 draw against Manchester United. Kyle Walker and a stunning goal from Sandro twice gave Tottenham Hotspur the lead. A Wayne Rooney penalty earned United a point. Vlad Chiriches and Lewis Holtby were on target as we beat Fulham 2-1 at Craven Cottage. More success away from home followed as an own goal and Paulinho secured a 2-1 win at Sunderland. Our unbeaten run came to an end as Liverpool beat 10-man Tottenham Hotspur 5-0. The Club parted company with Head Coach, Andre Villas-Boas, the following day. Tim Sherwood took control of the first team and an attacking line-up paid off at Southampton as Emmanuel Adebayor (2) and an own goal sealed a 3-2 win. Christian Eriksen scored a stunning free-kick, but Tottenham Hotspur were held at home to West Brom on Boxing Day. Stoke arrived three days later. A penalty from Roberto Soldado and goals from Mousa Dembele and Aaron Lennon moved Tottenham Hotspur to within three points off the top four.

JANUARY

Pld: 4 W: 3 D: 0 L: 1
End of month League table position: **fifth**

A second successive win at Old Trafford was the perfect start to 2014. Emmanuel Adebayor and Christian Eriksen were on target. After a disappointing FA Cup exit at Arsenal, we beat Crystal Palace 2-0 at White Hart Lane. Eriksen and Jermain Defoe, who had earlier announced his transfer to Toronto, were the goal scorers. Adebayor's superb form continued as we comfortably beat Swansea 3-1 at the Liberty Stadium. Two from the Togo international and a Chico Flores own goal put Spurs back in contention for a top four finish. We finished the month with a home defeat to Manchester City. The key moment in the game was Danny Rose's sending off, which was later overturned. The full-back was given a straight red card in the 49th minute after a tackle on Edin Dzeko inside the area, although he appeared to get good contact on the ball before the City striker went down. The visitors were only 1-0 up at that stage. City took full advantage, winning 5-1.

FEBRUARY

Pld: 4 W: 2 D: 1 L: 1
End of month League table position: **fifth**

February started with a trip to Hull – Paulinho levelled in the second half to earn a point. Emmanuel Adebayor's goal gave Tottenham Hotspur the points against an impressive Everton at White Hart Lane. One of our best performances of the season came just three days later at Newcastle. Adebayor (2), Paulinho and a stunning goal from Nacer Chadli sealed a superb 4-0 win. A second half goal from Robert Snodgrass was enough to give Norwich all three points at Carrow Road.

MARCH

Pld: 5 W: 2 D: 0 L: 3
End of month League table position: **sixth**

A first half goal from Roberto Soldado was enough to beat Cardiff at White Hart Lane. The following week Chelsea capitalised on a controversial sending off for Younes Kaboul at Stamford Bridge with the home side leading 1-0 at the time. Chelsea went on to win the match 4-0. A battling performance went unrewarded in the north London derby at White Hart Lane as a second-minute screamer from Tomas Rosicky was enough to clinch the victory for Arsenal. Gylfi Sigurdsson scored a stoppage time winner as we produced a magnificent fightback to overturn a 2-0 deficit against Southampton and snatch victory in the dying seconds. Christian Eriksen (2) levelled in the first half. Liverpool were the new favourites for the title after a 4-0 win over Tottenham Hotspur at Anfield.

APRIL

Pld: 4 W: 3 D: 1 L: 0
End of month League table position: **sixth**

The biggest win of the season arrived on a wet Monday night at White Hart Lane as a Christian Eriksen-inspired Tottenham Hotspur side thrashed Sunderland 5-1. Emmanuel Adebayor (2), Harry Kane, Eriksen and Gylfi Sigurdsson were all on target. A defeat looked on the cards as West Brom took a 3-0 first half lead at The Hawthorns. But an own goal, a Kane header and a stoppage time Eriksen goal rescued a point in an entertaining game. Kane was enjoying his extended run in the first team, scoring three goals in three games including one in our 3-1 win over Fulham at White Hart Lane. Paulinho and Younes Kaboul were also on target. Danny Rose scored the only goal of the game in a 1-0 win at Stoke to end April with a deserved victory.

MAY

Pld: 2 W: 1 D: 0 L: 1
Final League table position: sixth

West Ham United took full advantage of Younes Kaboul's first half red card, scoring twice before half time to win at Upton Park. Tottenham Hotspur secured European football after a comfortable final day win over Aston Villa. First half goals from Paulinho, an own goal and Emmanuel Adebayor sealed a 3-0 win to finish the season on 69 points.

OPTA STATS

18 players scored a Premier League goal for Tottenham Hotspur – a larger spread than any other team.

88% of matches won when Tottenham Hotspur have led – the highest proportion of any team.

21 – equalled their record number of League victories.

FINAL PREMIER LEAGUE TABLE

Pos	Team	P	GD	Pts
1	Manchester City	38	65	86
2	Liverpool	38	51	84
3	Chelsea	38	44	82
4	Arsenal	38	27	79
5	Everton	38	22	72
6	Tottenham Hotspur	38	4	69
7	Manchester United	38	21	64
8	Southampton	38	8	56
9	Stoke City	38	-7	50
10	Newcastle United	38	-16	49
11	Crystal Palace	38	-15	45
12	Swansea City	38	0	42
13	West Ham United	38	-11	40
14	Sunderland	38	-19	38
15	Aston Villa	38	-22	38
16	Hull City	38	-15	37
17	West Bromwich Albion	38	-16	36
18	Norwich City	38	-34	33
19	Fulham	38	-45	32
20	Cardiff City	38	-42	30

UEFA EUROPA LEAGUE REVIEW

Tottenham Hotspur were one of the early favourites to win the UEFA Europa League. After winning all six group matches, confidence grew at White Hart Lane. Our run came to an end in the last 16 to eventual finalists Benfica. The challenge now is to go all the way in the Europa League with Champions League football the reward for the 2015 winners.

UEFA EUROPA LEAGUE Play-off – First Leg

Dinamo Tbilisi 0-5 Tottenham Hotspur

This was the game where Andros Townsend officially burst onto the first team scene. The England international opened the scoring with a low strike from 20-yards after breaking up the pitch unchallenged in the 12th minute, and his assists for Paulinho and Roberto Soldado were equally as eye-catching. Townsend beat his defender on the right wing with ease before crossing for Paulinho, and the 22-year-old set up Soldado with a fantastic run and cross early on in the second half. Danny Rose scored with a stylish curled effort and Soldado grabbed his second of the match after a pinpoint cross from Chadli to secure a comfortable victory.

UEFA EUROPA LEAGUE Play-off – Second Leg

Tottenham Hotspur 3-0 Dinamo Tbilisi
(Tottenham Hotspur won 8-0 on aggregate)

Two goals from Jermain Defoe and a stunning effort from Lewis Holtby ensured a comfortable victory on a warm summer night at White Hart Lane.

UEFA EUROPA LEAGUE – Group K

Tottenham Hotspur 3-0 Tromso

Jermain Defoe closed to within two goals of becoming our joint top all-time European goalscorer and Christian Eriksen scored a superb first goal for us as we cruised to a 3-0 win over Norwegian outfit Tromso.

Anzhi 0-2 Tottenham Hotspur

Jermain Defoe made it seven goals in four starts in the season as Tottenham Hotspur dominated this match to take an early lead in the group. Nacer Chadli was also on target in Russia.

FC Sheriff 0-2 Tottenham Hotspur

Jermain Defoe equalled Martin Chivers' European goalscoring record for the club in spectacular fashion in the 2-0 win over FC Sheriff. Jan Vertonghen opened the scoring as we left Moldova with three points, nine so far in the group.

Tottenham Hotspur 2-1 FC Sheriff

Jermain Defoe became a record-breaker and Erik Lamela scored his first goal in a Spurs shirt as we booked our place in the knockout stages of the UEFA Europa League with a 2-1 defeat of FC Sheriff. Defoe's 23rd European goal for Tottenham Hotspur overtook club legend Martin Chivers, who was our half time guest.

Tromso 0-2 Tottenham Hotspur

Despite the freezing temperatures in Norway, Tottenham Hotspur left Tromso with three points. An own goal put Tottenham Hotspur ahead. Mousa Dembele added a second on 75 minutes.

Tottenham Hotspur 4-1 Anzhi

Roberto Soldado scored his first Tottenham Hotspur hat-trick to maintain our 100% record in the UEFA Europa League. Lewis Holtby was also on target at White Hart Lane.

UEFA EUROPA LEAGUE Round of 32 – First Leg

Dnipro 1-0 Tottenham Hotspur

Yevhen Konoplyanka scored the only goal from the penalty spot as Tottenham Hotspur lost 1-0 in Dnipro. Despite a poor pitch, the result was hard to take as we dominated for long periods. Dnipro were led by former Tottenham Hotspur manager Juande Ramos.

UEFA EUROPA LEAGUE Round of 32 – Second Leg

Tottenham Hotspur 3-1 Dnipro
(Tottenham Hotspur won 3-2 on aggregate)

It's hard to beat the atmosphere on European nights at White Hart Lane, and the magnificent support played their part in a stunning comeback, as goals from Christian Eriksen and two from Emmanuel Adebayor sealed our progress to the last 16.

UEFA EUROPA LEAGUE Last 16 – First Leg

Tottenham Hotspur 1-3 Benfica

Tottenham Hotspur faced a side who started the season in the UEFA Champions League and it was easy to see why Benfica were one of the favourites to win this tournament, as two goals from captain Luisao left Tottenham Hotspur with plenty to do in the second leg in Lisbon.

UEFA EUROPA LEAGUE Last 16 – Second Leg

Benfica 2-2 Tottenham Hotspur
(Benfica won 5-3 on aggregate)

If there was a match in the season where the score didn't reflect the story of the game – this was it. Benfica were clear favourites to advance to the quarter-finals after their comfortable win at White Hart Lane. Several first team regulars remained at home after a busy Premier League schedule, but the side selected for this game more than held their own. Despite the hosts taking a 4-1 aggregate lead through Ezequiel Garay in the first half, a quick-fire double from Nacer Chadli put us ahead on the night and just one goal from extra time. Harry Kane was brought down in the box, but claims for a penalty were waved away, before Benfica settled the tie with a 93rd-minute penalty from Lima. Our European challenge was over for another campaign.

DOMESTIC CUPS REVIEW
2013/2014

FA CUP – Third Round
Arsenal 2-0 Tottenham Hotspur

Our FA Cup adventure came to an early end in the north London derby. Santi Cazorla's first half strike was added to when Tomas Rosicky made the most of a defensive error.

CAPITAL ONE CUP – Third Round
Aston Villa 0-4 Tottenham Hotspur

It was the third game in just six days for Tottenham Hotspur, but they brushed aside Aston Villa in style at Villa Park. Jermain Defoe scored twice; his first, a clever finish after a brilliant looping through-ball from Lewis Holtby. Paulinho and Nacer Chadli were also on target.

CAPITAL ONE CUP – Fourth Round

Tottenham Hotspur 2-2 Hull City

(after extra time Tottenham Hotspur won 8-7 on penalties)

Tottenham Hotspur won their first penalty shoot-out since 1994 after an entertaining fourth round tie against Hull. Gylfi Sigurdsson had fired us ahead in the 16th minute with a truly stunning goal, before Curtis Davies' close-range shot deflected in off Brad Friedel to level it up nine minutes after the interval. Neither side could find a winner in normal time, but the visitors were in front on 99 minutes through Paul McShane, only for Harry Kane to force a penalty shoot-out when he equalised 10 minutes later. Brad Friedel saved two penalties to send us through to the quarter-final.

CAPITAL ONE CUP – Fifth Round

Tottenham Hotspur 1-2 West Ham United

Emmanuel Adebayor hit a fine goal on his return to the starting line-up, but two goals in the final 10 minutes saw West Ham United end our run in the Capital One Cup.

OUR GREAT DANE

It's hard to believe Eriksen is still in his early 20s given the key role he played at Ajax and now Spurs. When Gareth Bale stood behind a ball waiting for his free-kick to be taken, supporters were getting used to seeing it hit the back of the net, but they haven't had to wait too long to find a player just as devastating from a set-piece, as West Brom, Dnipro and Benfica found out last season.

He is now an important part of Mauricio Pochettino's plans for the long-term future. He won three Eredivisie titles during his Ajax career and he's hungry for more success at White Hart Lane.

After an impressive debut season for Tottenham Hotspur, Christian Eriksen is now a key player at White Hart Lane. The Denmark international collected the 2014 Player of the Year award, voted for by supporters. It was a hat-trick of awards for Christian, who was then presented with both the One Hotspur Members' and Junior Members' trophies, before the end of last season.

He was also named Danish Player of the Year by Denmark's equivalent of the PFA. Christian ended with 10 goals in 36 appearances in all competitions, including seven goals and eight assists in 25 matches in the Premier League.

"I was really honoured to receive these awards in my first season at the Club. It's always good that the fans enjoy what you are doing and that's the reason they go to the stadium, to be entertained and hopefully see us win. I'm pleased the supporters like what I've been doing and that I've been able to give them something back".

Eriksen was one of seven new signings in summer 2013. Naturally, some settled in earlier than others, but he took to the Premier League with ease and has proved to be great value at £11 million. Christian believes his love of London was a factor in his impressive start at the Lane.

"I really like it here. It's a nice, warm Club. I settled down quickly and eventually got used to driving on the left side of the road! We were taught English at school and then you come here and there's a few words you don't really understand. You really have to concentrate when you listen!"

2013/2014 STATS

Games – 36	Shots – 63
Goals – 10	Passes – 1,549
Assists – 10	Crosses – 242

ERIK LAMELA

After Mauricio Pochettino's appointment as Tottenham Hotspur Head Coach, one of the many tasks he set himself was to get the best out of this exceptional talent. Erik's debut season in England was disrupted due to injuries which hampered his progress in the 2013/2014 Season.

Due to that injury, Erik missed out on a place in Argentina's World Cup squad in Brazil. He continued his extensive rehabilitation throughout the summer. Erik was fit to start pre-season training and impressed on our tour of the United States and Canada.

Pochettino was aware of Erik's ability in Argentina and then followed his progression in Italy.

Despite a tough first season, there were still signs Spurs had signed a player of huge potential. Notably, his assist for Paulinho's stoppage-time winner at Cardiff. A goal, and man of the match performance against FC Sheriff and a clever through ball for Roberto Soldado against Anzhi.

In pre-season, Pochettino allowed Lamela the attacking freedom he enjoyed at Roma. Starting on the right, Erik is equally effective in the number 10 role, working well with team-mates under Pochettino's exciting attacking philosophy.

Erik is now aiming to follow in the footsteps of Spurs legends and compatriots Ossie Ardiles and Ricky Villa. If Lamela continues to show the commitment he has displayed since his arrival, Spurs fans will witness a new White Hart Lane superstar.

"I think I can play better than I did last season and I hope this happens for me and for the Spurs fans. I would love to do well for them."

MAURICIO POCHETTINO

Appointed as our Head Coach in May, 2014, Mauricio built his coaching reputation in Spain with RCD Espanyol before making his mark in the Premier League during an 18-month spell with Southampton.

Mauricio enjoyed a highly successful playing career, making his debut in 1988 with Argentinian side Newell's Old Boys at the age of 16 and winning the Argentine Primera División with them in 1991.

He embarked on the first of two playing spells with La Liga outfit Espanyol in 1994, helping his side to Copa del Rey success in his final full season with them before joining Paris Saint-Germain in January, 2001.

Having been a regular starter for the French giants, he switched to Bordeaux in 2003 before rejoining Espanyol on loan mid-way through the 2003-04 campaign - a move made permanent later in 2004.

He called time on his playing career in 2006 having won a second Copa del Rey title with Espanyol and achieved 20 international caps with Argentina.

"This is a Club with tremendous history and prestige and I am honoured to have been given this opportunity to be its Head Coach."

He returned to Espanyol as Head Coach in January, 2009, winning admirers across Europe for his high pressing attacking brand of football as well as for prioritising the development of young players from the side's youth setup.

He departed in November, 2012, after almost four years in charge, and was appointed First Team Manager at Southampton in January, 2013.

He guided the Saints to an eighth place finish last season - their highest ever in the Premier League - before his arrival in N17.

"Tottenham Hotspur has a huge following across the world and I have great admiration for the passion the fans show for this team. We are determined to give the supporters the kind of attacking football and success that we are all looking to achieve."

Hugo **Lloris**

The France captain is now in his third season at the club. Hugo captained his country for the first time in November 2010 against England at Wembley. He is considered one of the best goalkeepers in the Premier League.

Michel **Vorm**

The Dutch international goalkeeper joined Spurs from Swansea last summer. Michel made 97 appearances for Swansea and was also part of the Netherlands' World Cup squad in Brazil.

PLAYER PROFILES

Brad **Friedel**

Brad holds the record for consecutive starts in the Premier League. Vastly experienced on the pitch, he is also a club ambassador with a particular focus on our work with his native United States.

Younes **Kaboul**

Younes returned to the first team last season after missing the entire 2012/2013 campaign through injury. When fit, Younes is an important member of the first team, and has also captained the side.

Jan **Vertonghen**

Jan is a key member of the first team. The Belgium international impressed during the 2014 World Cup. The versatile centre-back is also accomplished at left-back. Jan was awarded a place in the PFA's Premier League Team of the Season for 2012/2013, voted for by his peers.

Kyle **Naughton**

Kyle's versatility saw him feature in 34 League and cup matches last season. Kyle joined us with fellow full-back Kyle Walker from Sheffield United in July 2009 having played 50 times for the Bramall Lane side in 2008/2009.

Ben **Davies**

The exciting young Welsh left-back joined Spurs in July 2014. Ben impressed at Swansea last season establishing himself as the first choice left-back for club and country.

Federico **Fazio**

Federico joined Spurs from Sevilla in August. The Argentina international made 194 appearances for the La Liga side and was also a key member of their Europa League-winning team last season, beating Benfica on penalties in the final in Turin.

Eric **Dier**

Eric joined Spurs from Sporting Lisbon in July last summer. The England Under-21 international moved to Portugal with his family aged six and impressed at Sporting's academy, eventually becoming a first team regular last season. Eric is comfortable anywhere across the back four and in a defensive midfield role.

Danny **Rose**

Danny started out at Spurs as a left winger, but after impressing at left-back for England U21s and Sunderland during a loan spell, he became our first choice in that position last season.

PLAYER PROFILES

Kyle **Walker**

The England international was restricted to 34 appearances in League and cup competitions after a pelvic injury saw him miss the latter part of the season and the 2014 World Cup. Kyle was named PFA Young Player of the Year in 2011/2012.

Aaron **Lennon**

Aaron is now in his 10th season at the club. The winger made 33 appearances for Spurs last season. Aaron joined us as an 18-year-old from hometown club Leeds United in July 2005 and burst onto the scene during his maiden campaign.

Etienne **Capoue**

The French international midfielder joined us from Toulouse in August 2013. Etienne made an immediate impression against Crystal Palace and Swansea at the start of last season, but a serious ankle injury disrupted his campaign and he subsequently missed the 2014 World Cup.

Paulinho

The Brazilian international midfielder scored eight goals from midfield in his debut season in the Premier League. Paulinho joined Spurs from Corinthians in July 2013.

Mousa **Dembele**

Mousa is now in his third season at White Hart Lane. He featured for Belgium in the 2014 World Cup. Mousa joined Spurs from Fulham in August 2012.

Nabil **Bentaleb**

Nabil enjoyed an unforgettable 2014, breaking into the Spurs first team and playing a key role in Algeria reaching the second round of the World Cup. He is a successful product of the Spurs academy.

Benjamin **Stambouli**

Benjamin joined Spurs from Montpellier in September. The midfielder made his senior debut with the French side in 2010 and went on to make 129 First Team appearances in all competitions, scoring four goals.

Christian **Eriksen**

The Danish playmaker scored 10 goals and created 10 assists in his first season at White Hart Lane, winning our Player of the Year award for 2013/2014. Christian won three consecutive Dutch league championships with Ajax between 2011 and 2013.

PLAYER PROFILES

Andros **Townsend**

Lightning winger Andros Townsend is another Academy graduate to make an impressive transition to first team football at Spurs. Andros is now a regular in the England squad and scored a brilliant goal against Montenegro in the World Cup qualifiers.

Harry **Kane**

Harry is now a permanent fixture in the first team after an impressive run at the end of season 2013/2014. The England Under-21 international scored three goals in three games in April 2014 in the Premier League.

Nacer **Chadli**

The Belgium international scored five goals in his debut season at White Hart Lane. Nacer is comfortable in any role behind the striker, but he was primarily on the left-hand side last season.

Roberto **Soldado**

Roberto scored 11 goals in 36 appearances in his first season at Spurs. The Spanish international joined the club from Valencia in the summer of 2013.

Emmanuel **Adebayor**

Emmanuel returned to the first team squad to score an impressive 14 goals in 25 appearances. The Togo international is now in his fourth season at Spurs.

TOTTENHAM HOTSPUR

SPOT THE BALL

Can you work out which is the real ball in the picture below?

Answer on Page 60

ANAGRAMS

How well do you know the Spurs team? See if you can unravel these anagrams to find the names of your favourite players.

1. So rough ill

2. Mover milch

3. Brief ladder

4. Okay nebulous

5. Even John Grant

6. Lay on the gunk

7. Beside van

8. Icier red

9. Darn nosey

10. Weekly lark

11. On ran on lane

12. A teenie pounce

13. Upon hail

14. Double same me

15. Able ant nibble

16. Inheritance risks

17. Snow and rodents

18. Chancier lad

19. Bolder toad or so

20. Amenable you dream

21. Rare hanky

Answers on Page 60

New Year's Day 2014

Two consecutive wins in two years at Old Trafford. Before that, Spurs had gone over 23 years without beating Manchester United on their home turf.

2

Adebayor (34), Eriksen (66)

33

HUGO LLORIS

Spurs fans have always appreciated a top goalkeeper at White Hart Lane and Hugo Lloris is the latest in a long line adored by the supporters. He commited his future to the Club after signing a new five-year contract in the summer.

The French international captain arrived from Lyon in August 2012 and is now in his third season at the Club. Despite some disappointing results last season, Lloris was a strong contender for our Player of the Year award.

Lloris is often described as a 'sweeper-keeper', patrolling his penalty area by closing down the attack and leaving his line quickly to avert any danger. Whilst his approach can at times be risky, it's a key skill that helps place him amongst the very best in the world.

"It's always difficult when you concede goals when you're a goalkeeper but you have to always stay mentally strong, keep a good spirit and work every day. It helps the team to get results."

HUGO LLORIS

After impressing for France during the World Cup in Brazil, Hugo was linked with the world's biggest clubs. Thankfully, all fears were quickly erased by signing his new deal.

"It's very important to feel at home at a club and for my family to feel well. I enjoy a great relationship with the Club and the fans. The arrival of Mauricio Pochettino was important as well.

"I trust the Club and I'm sure we will progress in a positive way. Last season wasn't the season we all hoped for but we were still able to finish sixth in the League. We know where we have to improve, the Club also knows and there is a feeling and a confident connection between the Club and the players."

After replacing Brad Friedel, who had broken a record of 310 straight Premier League starts, Hugo quickly adapted to English football, particularly the physical nature of the Premier League. He always looks comfortable when dealing with crosses thanks to his athleticism. Fans have consistently seen him put his body on the line. His bravery has never been questioned. Lloris is certainly not the tallest 'keeper in the League, but he makes up for that with his agility; a key component for a modern day number one.

Spurs have a goalkeeper only just entering his prime. Plenty of time to become a White Hart Lane legend.

"From day one, I knew he was a fantastic goalkeeper – a world-class goalkeeper – and I'm very happy to play alongside him at Spurs."

YOUNES KABOUL

NEW SIGNING

BENJAMIN STAMBOULI

Benjamin joined Spurs from Montpellier on transfer deadline day.
The 24-year-old was a key part of the Montpellier side that won the
French league championship in 2012. He also has 14 caps for the French
Under-21 national team to his name.

BEN DAVIES

Ben Davies joined Spurs from Swansea in the summer on a five-year contract. Ben arrived with former Swansea team-mate Michel Vorm. The Wales international was a popular signing with the supporters, adding further quality to the back four. Ben made his Spurs debut against Toronto during our pre-season tour of the United States and Canada.

Davies earned his first professional contract with Swansea in 2011 and developed into a key player for the first team, winning their Young Player of the Year accolade the past two seasons.

His impressive club form earned him a call-up to the Wales national side, where he is now a regular in Chris Coleman's squad. He made a total of 91 appearances for Swansea, including starting their League Cup Final win against Bradford City in 2013.

Tottenham have enjoyed great success with Welsh internationals in the past, more recently with Gareth Bale, and Davies revealed Bale often spoke of his love for Spurs during international duty. Ben admits it was hard to leave the club he had served so well from childhood, but a move to White Hart Lane was too good to turn down.

"I was very happy to be joining a club like Spurs. It was such a good opportunity for me and there was no doubt in my mind about it. It's a great place to be. The squad has been great to me, they were very welcoming and when you join a new squad, that makes it all the easier, when you are with such a good bunch of lads."

Ben's chance at Swansea arrived after an injury to first choice left-back Neil Taylor. At 19, he immediately impressed Swansea supporters and Manager Michael Laudrup with displays beyond his years. A League Cup winners medal capped a memorable first season for Davies. His technique, positional sense and ability to drive forward made him an ideal choice for Head Coach Mauricio Pochettino. In an era where attacking full-backs are the popular choice, Spurs secured a player who is also skilled in the art of defending. And, after more successful passes than any other left-back in the Premier League last season, Spurs have a high quality 'Mr Reliable' for many years to come.

"Ben has a lot of potential. He's very humble and a great guy. I think he fits into the team perfectly, especially the way Spurs like to play."

MICHEL VORM

NEW SIGNING
FEDERICO FAZIO

Federico joined Spurs from Sevilla in August on a four-year contract. Federico made 194 appearances for Sevilla and was a key member of the team that won the UEFA Europa League last season, beating Benfica on penalties in the final. He also won the FIFA Under-20 World Cup with Argentina in 2007 and followed up with Olympic gold in Beijing a year later.

Federico says moving to Spurs was an easy decision to make.

"England is a very good country and I choose Tottenham, an amazing Club. This is the best for me.

"The Premier League is the best in the world. This is a new experience for me. I watch the Premier League on TV and I'm very happy to be here at Tottenham."

Did you know: Federico studied medicine before his career in professional football.

MICHEL VORM

Michel joined Spurs after three successful seasons at Swansea. The Netherlands international goalkeeper arrived on a four-year contract in July.

Despite Spurs already boasting France international Hugo Lloris and the experienced Brad Friedel, Michel said his move to White Hart Lane was an easy decision.

"It is one of the best Clubs in the Premier League. I'm delighted to play for a team like Spurs. The facilities are fantastic and potential of the squad is huge. I've worked with a lot of goalkeepers in the past and at this level it's good to have so much competition."

Vorm moved to Swansea in August 2011 in their debut season in the Premier League. His impressive debut season in England saw him pick up Supporters' Player of the Year, Players' Player and the Away Player trophies at their end of season awards. In total, he made 97 appearances for Swansea and was also part of the Netherlands' World Cup squad who finished third last summer in Brazil.

Michel, similar to Hugo, is extremely agile and comfortable on the ball. His quick reactions helped him pull off stunning saves during his time at Swansea. At 31, Michel's experience is invaluable for our younger players and with Hugo and Brad, Spurs have one of the strongest set of goalkeepers in the Premier League.

ERIC DIER

The England Under-21 international defender joined us on a five-year contract from Sporting Lisbon in summer 2014. He enjoyed a dream League debut, scoring a stoppage-time winner against West Ham at Upton Park to stun the home side and get Mauricio Pochettino's reign as Tottenham Hotspur Head Coach off to the perfect start.

Eric's background is very different to other young English defenders. He moved to Portugal with his family when he was six. He was spotted by Sporting Lisbon two years later and progressed through the ranks, becoming a regular in the first team before his departure.

Despite feeling at home in Portugal, the versatile defender admits his ambition was to return home and play in the Premier League.

"It's a strange background, everyone seems surprised by it, it's 'an Englishman abroad' but I didn't go abroad for football, it just happened that way.

"I moved there with my family and then football got involved in my life and I went through Sporting's youth team like anyone would here.

"Initially it was hard because I didn't speak the language, so that made it tough and I was seen as a bit of an outsider when I was younger but once I picked up the language it was really easy. I was one of them really.

"It's always been my ambition, my dream to come back to England and play in the Premier League so I'm really happy to be back."

Eric's progression caught the eye of England and a number of Premier League clubs. Despite spending a short period on loan at Everton when he was 17, Eric considers Spurs to be the perfect club for him.

"Spurs is a massive Club, I've known about them since I was young and always enjoyed the way they play, the attacking football and coming from Portugal, that will suit me."

Eric has represented England at Under-18, Under-19, Under-20 and Under-21 level. On his Sporting debut, he provided an assist against Braga, later receiving a standing ovation from his supporters. At 6ft 2in tall, Dier is the perfect size for a Premier League defender, but his ability to play anywhere across the back four will make him a key part of the squad for his debut season.

OUR BEST JUNIOR MEMBERSHIP EVER!

TOTTENHAM HOTSPUR

LOTS OF **NEW** EXCLUSIVE BENEFITS

BE PART OF THE TEAM
WELCOME TO OUR WORLD

JOIN OUR WORLD NOW!
tottenhamhotspur.com/juniors

Jesus Perez
Assistant Head Coach

Miguel D'Agostino
First Team Coach

JESUS PEREZ

Jesus followed Mauricio Pochettino to Spurs after a successful spell as Southampton Assistant Manager. Jesus also worked alongside our Head Coach at Espanyol as Fitness Coach. Born in Spain, Jesus has coached for 18 years at Al Ittihad, Almeria, Rayo Vallecano, Pontevedra, Real Murcia, Castellon and Tarragona.

MIGUEL D'AGOSTINO

Miguel also followed Mauricio Pochettino to White Hart Lane from Southampton. He played alongside Pochettino for Argentinian side Newell's Old Boys in the early 1990s. After leaving French side Brest as Chief Scout, he joined Pochettino's coaching staff at Espanyol.

TONI JIMENEZ

Toni was appointed Goalkeeping Coach in the summer of 2014. After leaving Barcelona, he had a brief spell at Rayo Vallecano, before making over 200 appearances for Espanyol, where he met then team-mate Mauricio Pochettino. Toni won three caps for Spain and won a gold medal for Spain in the 1992 Olympics. Toni returned to Espanyol as Assistant Coach to Mauricio, before following him to Southampton and then Tottenham Hotspur.

Toni Jiménez
Goalkeeping Coach

INTERNATIONAL SPURS

International breaks at Hotspur Way can be a quiet time with many of the team away playing for their country. As you can see, Spurs have many international players, from all over the world.

1. Christian Eriksen - Denmark
2. Andros Townsend – England
3. Kyle Walker – England
4. Etienne Capoue – France
5. Erik Lamela – Argentina
6. Federico Fazio – Argentina
7. Ben Davies – Wales
8. Roberto Soldado – Spain
9. Vlad Chiriches – Romania
10. Emmanuel Adebayor – Togo

Spurs had eight representatives on World Cup duty in Brazil.

11. Nabil Bentaleb – Algeria
12. Jan Vertonghen – Belgium
13. Mousa Dembele – Belgium
14. Nacer Chadli – Belgium
15. Paulinho – Brazil
16. Hugo Lloris – France
17. Michel Vorm – Netherlands

TOTTENHAM HOTSPUR
LEGENDS

Do you want to know why Tottenham Hotspur is such a special Club? Regardless of league positions, Spurs have always attracted world class talent. Some developed into White Hart Lane legends. In 2014 we remembered Jimmy Greaves, Jurgen Klinsmann, Dave Mackay, Ricky Villa and Pat Jennings. Below are five more greats who have graced the White Hart Lane turf.

Steve Perryman (above)

Steve Perryman played over 850 matches in all competitions for Spurs and currently holds the record for most appearances in the League, FA Cup, League Cup and Europe.

In May 2012 Steve was inducted into our Hall of Fame. He has won more medals than any other player at White Hart Lane with two UEFA Cups, two FA Cups and two League Cups alongside the honour of the Football Writers' Player of the Year in 1982.

Perryman made his league debut in 1969 and departed in 1986, after a memorable career at the Club. Steve was named captain in 1975. He returned to the Club as assistant manager under Ossie Ardiles in 1993/1994. Steve is currently Director of Football at Exeter City.

Danny Blanchflower (right)

Danny was an inspirational captain and a huge part of our Double winning side. He is one of the greatest players in the Club's history. Danny lifted the League Championship in 1961, FA Cup in 1961 and 1962 and the UEFA Cup Winners' Cup in 1963. Danny made 382 appearances for Spurs, retiring at the end of the 1963/1964 Season. Danny's famous quote is still heavily ingrained in our Club's philosophy: "The great fallacy is that the game is first and last about winning. It's nothing of the kind. The game is about glory. It is about doing things in style, with a flourish, about going out and beating the other lot, not waiting for them to die of boredom."

Ossie Ardiles (below)

Ossie's move to White Hart Lane shocked the football world. He joined, with Argentina team-mate Ricky Villa after the 1978 World Cup. Ossie was part of a Spurs side that won two FA Cups and the UEFA Cup in 1984 and will also be remembered for his role in the 1981 FA Cup Final song, 'Ossie's Dream'. Ossie went on to make 221 appearances for Spurs. He returned to manage the Club in 1993/1994 and briefly in 1994/1995.

Ossie is still a regular at White Hart Lane, paying particular attention to fellow countrymen Mauricio Pochettino and Erik Lamela.

Teddy Sheringham (above)

Our former captain made 276 First Team appearances in a Spurs shirt during two spells with the Club, scoring 124 goals. Teddy joined Spurs from Nottingham Forest in 1992. It was one of the signings of the season, as Teddy won the inaugural Premier League Golden Boot award with 22 goals. Teddy represented England during his Spurs career, playing a key role, as the Three Lions reached the Euro '96 semi-final. He joined Manchester United in 1997, but returned to the Club in 2001 and was quickly named Club captain. Teddy was inducted into the Spurs Hall of Fame in May 2008.

Martin Chivers (right)

Martin is one of our most successful strikers at White Hart Lane. He scored 202 goals in 415 games. 'Big Chiv' joined Spurs in January 1968, for a then Club-record fee of £125,000. He played a big part in adding two trophies to the cabinet, scoring both goals against Aston Villa in the 1971 League Cup Final and another double in the 1972 UEFA Cup Final against Wolves. Chivers scored 22 goals in 32 European appearances, a record only beaten by Jermain Defoe in November 2013. He is still a regular at the Lane on matchdays where he is a popular member of our hospitality team. Martin was inducted into the Spurs Hall of Fame in April 2007.

RISING STARS

In a popular feature we profile five players who could set White Hart Lane alight in the future.

MILOS VELJKOVIC

Milos was born and raised in Basel, Switzerland but represents Serbia at international level. He is a talented central defender/holding midfielder. His form as a holding midfielder in the development squad regularly earned him a place in the first team squad towards the end of last season, going on as a substitute in our wins against Sunderland and Aston Villa.

Milos has been capped at Under-17, – 18 and – 19 levels for Serbia. Milos was a regular in our starting XI during our pre-season tour of the United States.

ALEX PRITCHARD

The young midfielder earned rave reviews for his performances during a season-long loan with League One side Swindon Town in 2013/2014. He featured 44 times and scored six goals.

His eye-catching displays were such that he was nominated in two categories at the end-of-season Football League awards – League One Player of the Season and Football League Young Player of the Year. Although he missed out in the final reckoning in both, it still showed he had made quite an impression at the County Ground.

Alex featured twice in the U20s 2013 World Cup in Turkey – his first England caps at any level.

Alex made his Tottenham Hotspur debut as an 83rd minute substitute in our last match of the 2013/2014 campaign against Aston Villa. He is currently on loan at Championship side Brentford.

RYAN FREDERICKS

The attacking full-back impressed in our Europa League tie against Anzhi at White Hart Lane in December 2013. Ryan spent the second half of the season on loan at Millwall. Born in Hammersmith, London, Ryan made his breakthrough at Spurs in 2011/2012, when he made his debut in the Europa League play-off against Hearts in August 2011. He went on to make three first-team appearances in Europe.

He joined our Academy in July 2009 and signed professional forms in July 2010. Ryan started his Spurs career in a more attacking role and scored seven goals in 16 appearances for our Under-18s in 2009/2010. Ryan is currently on loan at Middlesbrough.

KENNY MCEVOY

Kenny is a highly-rated young winger who joined our Academy in July 2011. He impressed in the NextGen series and is now established in our Under-21 side.

Kenny's ability to play on either wing saw him travel with the first team squad during Spurs' 2013/2014 Europa League campaign. Born in Waterford, Republic of Ireland, Kenny has earned caps at Under-16, – 17, – 19 and recently at Under-21 level for the Republic of Ireland. Kenny is currently on loan at League One side Peterborough United.

JOSHUA ONOMAH

A talented prospect. Joshua was an unused substitute for our Europa League last 32 tie at Dnipro in 2013/2014, at the age of 16. He enjoyed success representing England in the Under-17 European Championships last summer.

Joshua is a central attacking midfielder who was born and raised in Enfield. He's already a regular in our Under-21 side despite his young age.

WORDSEARCH

Can you find the names of NINE Spurs legends that featured in the Ledley King Testimonial? Words can go horizontally, vertically and diagonally in any direction.

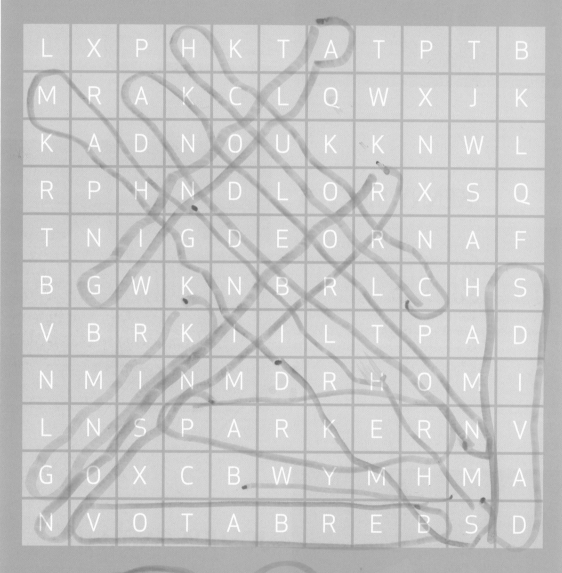

L	X	P	H	K	T	A	T	P	T	B
M	R	A	K	C	L	Q	W	X	J	K
K	A	D	N	O	U	K	K	N	W	L
R	P	H	N	D	L	O	R	X	S	Q
T	N	I	G	D	E	O	R	N	A	F
B	G	W	K	N	B	R	L	C	H	S
V	B	R	K	I	I	L	T	P	A	D
N	M	I	N	M	D	R	H	O	M	I
L	N	S	P	A	R	K	E	R	N	V
G	O	X	C	B	W	Y	M	H	M	A
N	V	O	T	A	B	R	E	B	S	D

Anderton   Davids   Parker

Berbatov   Ginola   Robinson

Crouch   King   Sheringham

Answers on Page 60

Spurs enjoyed a successful tour of the United States and Canada during the summer. Fitness was the key, with double training sessions for the players. Fans were already witnessing Mauricio Pochettino's style and influence during the three-match tour. We were delighted to see a large number of our American-based supporters' clubs in attendance.

Seattle Sounders 3-3 Tottenham Hotspur

In Mauricio Pochettino's first game in charge, we came up against one of the strongest sides in Major League Soccer (MLS). We were also re-united with former Spurs forward Clint Dempsey. Lewis Holtby put us ahead on 10 minutes before a Gonzalo Pineda penalty and Osvaldo Alonso's stunning effort either side of half-time gave the home side the upper hand.

But two Spurs penalties from substitutes Roberto Soldado and Yago Falque, either side of a Tristan Bowen tap-in, made for a lively second half. Over 55,000 fans witnessed an entertaining friendly. DeAndre Yedlin featured for Seattle.

Toronto 2-3 Tottenham Hotspur

Erik Lamela scored twice as Spurs were victorious against Ryan Nelsen's Toronto, who were captained by former White Hart Lane favourite Jermain Defoe. Toronto levelled in the second half before Andros Townsend scored an impressive winner. Ben Davies made his debut after joining the Club from Swansea.

Spurs vs Seattle Sounders at CenturyLink Field, Seattle, USA (above).

Spurs vs Chicago Fire, Toyota Park, Bridgeview, USA (above, right).

Erik Lamela celebrates scoring his side's third goal vs Toronto with teammate Ben Davies (right).

Chicago 0-2 Tottenham Hotspur

We completed a successful pre-season tour of the United States and Canada with a solid 2-0 victory over Chicago Fire at Toyota Park, thanks to goals in either half from Harry Kane and Aaron Lennon. Under-21 regulars Ryan Fredericks, Miloš Veljković and academy goalkeeper Luke McGee featured.

Lewis Holtby takes selfie with fans at Spurs vs Toronto friendly in BMO Field, Toronto, Canada (above).

vs Celtic @ Helsinki Olympic Stadium, Finland (left).

Celebrating Soldado's goal against FC Schalke (below).

Celtic 1-6 Tottenham Hotspur

A young Celtic side were outclassed in our penultimate pre-season friendly in Helsinki. First-half goals from Harry Kane, Roberto Soldado and Lewis Holtby, topped up by second half strikes from Erik Lamela, Christian Eriksen and an Emmanuel Adebayor penalty, settled a one-sided contest in which the team dominated from start to finish. Once again, Spurs were well supported by fans based in Finland.

Tottenham Hotspur 2-1 FC Schalke 04

A goal in each half from strikers Emmanuel Adebayor and Roberto Soldado ensured our pre-season campaign ended in victory as we defeated FC Schalke 04 2-1. Ex-Spur Kevin-Prince Boateng was on target for Schalke. Eric Dier was impressive on his debut, playing the full 90 minutes.

THE SPURS QUIZ

It's a grand old team to play for and it's a grand old team to see, so if you know your history, try this 2015 Spurs Quiz!

1. Where did Spurs finish in the 2013/2014 Season?

2. Jurgen Klinsmann first joined Spurs from which club?

3. Erik Lamela represents which nation?

4. Name our matchday club mascot.

5. Name our opponents in Group K in the 2013/2014 UEFA Europa League.

6. Who was our top goalscorer in 2013/2014?

7. Who were our opponents in the 1961 FA Cup Final?

8. Name Mauricio Pochettino's backroom staff.

9. Mauricio Pochettino represented which nation as a player?

10. Who did we beat in the 2008 Carling Cup Final?

11. Name the three Tottenham Hotspur players who represented Belgium at the 2014 FIFA World Cup.

12. How many European trophies have we won as at August 2014?

13. True or false – Tottenham Hotspur signed Robbie Keane from Inter Milan.

14. Christian Eriksen represents which nation?

15. Who did we face on the opening day this season?

Answers on Page 61

3

GOAL OF THE SEASON
2013/2014

Thousands of you took time to vote both on **tottenhamhotspur.com** and via **@SpursOfficial** on Twitter.

Here are the top 10.

Goal 1 – Danny Rose v Dinamo Tbilisi

The full-back hit a powerful left-footed shot over the Tbilisi 'keeper and into the top corner from 20 yards out. The strike even had the Dinamo fans applauding.

Goal 2 – Lewis Holtby v Dinamo Tbilisi

Jermain Defoe and Tom Carroll worked the ball out to Holtby 25 yards from goal. He drilled a rising right-foot shot which clipped the underside of the crossbar as it flew into the back of the net. Holtby's first goal in our colours.

Goal 3 – Christian Eriksen v Tromso

Defoe gathered Paulinho's crossfield pass on the byline and laid it back to the supporting Kyle Naughton, who in turn popped infield to Eriksen. The Dane looked up and hit a superb 25-yard right-foot shot which curled up and over the Tromso 'keeper and into the far corner, a delightful way to open his account in our colours.

4

Goal 4 – Gylfi Sigurdsson v Hull City

Kyle Naughton played the ball into Sigurdsson 25 yards from goal, he turned Curtis Davies with a neat flick and smashed a rising drive which flew past Jakupovic. A truly stunning goal.

5

Goal 5 – Sandro v Manchester Utd

Sandro picked up the ball 30 yards from goal, cut inside Cleverley, beat the United man again and then hit a vicious right-foot shot which flew into the top corner.

Goal 6 – Lewis Holtby v Fulham

Holtby took charge after receiving the ball on the corner of the area, he then dribbled across and unleashed a belter that defeated Stekelenburg and flew high into the net to secure a 2-1 victory.

Goal 9 – Nacer Chadli v Newcastle Utd

Chadli hit the goal of the night, a 25-yard curler that buried into the top corner as Tottenham Hotspur beat Newcastle 4-0 at St James' Park.

Goal 7 – Emmanuel Adebayor v West Ham Utd

Andros Townsend picked the ball up five yards outside our box and slid it down the line to Defoe. He burst away from O'Brien and sent over a cross which fell invitingly for Adebayor, who smashed it first time past Adrian and in off the crossbar to send the Lane into raptures.

Goal 10 – Gylfi Sigurdsson v Southampton

A deep free-kick from Lloris was headed away by Fonte, only as far as Eriksen who touched the ball square to Sigurdsson. He drilled a 25-yard shot into the bottom corner and the home crowd erupted.

Goal 8 – Christian Eriksen v West Bromwich Albion

A first Premier League goal for Eriksen. The Dane's 22-yard free kick crashed in off the underside of the bar.

AND THE WINNER IS...

Gylfi's fantastic strike against Hull City in the Capital One Cup on October 30 – a quick turn and thunderbolt into the top corner – won the poll. Gylfi joined Swansea last summer, after two seasons at White Hart Lane.

Sandro's 25-yarder against Manchester United was second and Christian Eriksen's against Tromso was placed third.

LEDLEY KING TESTIMONIAL

SPURS 3-6 LEDLEY GUEST XI

It was an occasion fit for a King at White Hart Lane as we paid tribute to our legendary former captain Ledley King in some style.

There was an amazing turnout from team-mates past and present as well as fantastic support from our fans who filled the Lane, all wanting to pay tribute to a true Spurs great.

A full house was treated to an entertaining game featuring a glittering array of Spurs stars from our recent history, including the likes of Teddy Sheringham, Darren Anderton, Dimitar Berbatov, David Ginola, Peter Crouch, Edgar Davids and, of course, the return to action of Ledley himself at centre-half. And while the scoreline was immaterial, the fans were delighted to see Ledley's Guest XI score six times, with Louis Saha helping himself to a hat-trick and Sheringham netting a brace.

Ledley's side were awarded a penalty after Younes Kaboul and Michael Dawson bundled King over inside the area and the man of the moment, of course, stepped up to take the penalty.

Ledley popped the ball into the net past Friedel, who would surely have been the villain of the piece had he saved the spot-kick!

"I always said he was one of the best defenders in the world. I've played with many and against a lot and I can tell he's one of the best."

Edgar Davids, Tottenham Hotspur 2005-2007

Darren Anderton, Tottenham Hotspur 1992-2004

Spurs XI were given the chance to equalise when Emmanuel Adebayor was brought down by a combination of Michael Brown and King and the referee awarded another spot-kick. Ade beat Neil Sullivan with a twice-taken penalty... to the disappointment of the crowd!

Ginola and Berbatov were proving to the crowd that class is permanent. Present squad members also showcased some delightful skill. Christian Eriksen lifted the ball onto the back of his neck and ran forwards, before Ledley's XI regained their lead.

There was a goal made in Spurs heaven – as Anderton released Berbatov down the right, he advanced on goal before sliding the perfect ball for Sheringham to run onto and hit right-footed first time past Friedel.

Then just moments before half-time, Friedel blocked Anderton's shot after some neat footwork from the midfielder and Sheringham tapped home the rebound to make it 3-1 at the break.

Boris Johnson, Mayor of London

Young striker Nathan Oduwa latched onto a throughball and dinked a lovely finish over 'England's No. 1' Paul Robinson to reduce the deficit to 3-2. Louis Saha scored his first of the evening to make it 4-2. Then on 56 minutes Ledley departed the White Hart Lane pitch for what is likely to be the very last time. The entire stadium and both sets of players gave him the send-off he so richly deserves as he took his place on the bench. Saha then scored his second of the evening to make it 5-2.

Etienne Capoue reduced the deficit again on 76 minutes with a 25-yard effort low into the far corner to make it 5-3, before we were 'treated' to some deft touches on the ball from referee Howard Webb, although that was swiftly brought to an end by a tackle from behind by Holtby. Amazingly, no card was shown!

Saha ended the occasion by smashing home a sixth for Ledley's team, the last kick of a wonderful game and fantastic night.

Player, Captain, Ambassador, Legend... the perfect tribute to a genuine Spurs great.

Spurs: Friedel (Archer 46), Naughton (Fredericks 46), Dawson (A McQueen 46), Kaboul (Ogilvie 46, Lesniak 73), Fryers (Walker-Peters 46), McEvoy (McEneff 46), Sandro (Capoue 46), Veljkovic (Holtby 46), Eriksen (Pritchard 46), Adebayor (Oduwa 46), Obika (Miller 57). Substitute (not used): Lameiras.

Ledley XI: Sullivan (Robinson 46, Parks 80), Brown (Young 46), King (Bassong 56), Perry (Chimbonda 46, Thelwell 76), Taricco (Stalteri 46), Anderton (Fox 46), Parker (Tainio 16, Freund 61), Davids (Palacios 46), Ginola (Davies 46), Berbatov (Saha 46), Sheringham (Crouch 46).

Goals: Spurs – Adebayor (pen), Oduwa, Capoue; **Ledley's XI** – King (pen), Sheringham (2), Saha (3).

GUESS THE GAME

Welcome to a new and exciting feature. Tottenham Hotspur have had many memorable victories, but can you guess the particular game using the match commentary?

1. "This is a strong counter-attack from Spurs. Aaron Lennon with the ball now, he's beaten the left-back, it's still Lennon... he's found Crouch. Goal for Spurs!"

2. "Is Gascoigne going to have a crack? He is you know. Oh I say! That is schoolboys' own stuff."

3. "Defoe gets past Ferdinand. That's a good reverse pass, Bale shoots, it's saved by De Gea, but Dempsey is there first to restore Tottenham's two-goal advantage."

4. "Van der Vaart with the free-kick. Kaboul with the header, it's 3-2! The comeback is complete!"

Answers on Page 61

QUIZ ANSWERS

Spot the Ball Page 30

Anagrams Page 31

1. Hugo Lloris
2. Michel Vorm
3. Brad Friedel
4. Younes Kaboul
5. Jan Vertonghen
6. Kyle Naughton
7. Ben Davies
8. Eric Dier
9. Danny Rose
10. Kyle Walker
11. Aaron Lennon

12. Etienne Capoue
13. Paulinho
14. Mousa Dembele
15. Nabil Bentaleb
16. Christian Eriksen
17. Andros Townsend
18. Nacer Chadli
19. Roberto Soldado
20. Emmanuel Adebayor
21. Harry Kane

Wordsearch Page 48

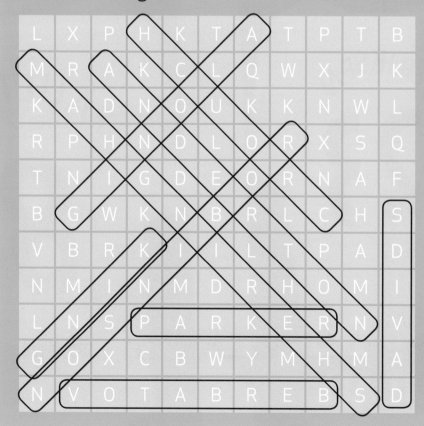

The Spurs Quiz Page 52

Guess the Game Page 58

1

2

PETER CROUCH
15 February, 2011 – AC Milan 0-1 Tottenham Hotspur

PAUL GASCOIGNE'S FREE-KICK
14 April, 1991 – Tottenham Hotspur 3-1 Arsenal

3

4

CLINT DEMPSEY
29 September, 2012
– Manchester United 2-3 Tottenham Hotspur

YOUNES KABOUL
20 November, 2010 – Arsenal 2-3 Tottenham Hotspur